TALKING ABOUT
Racism

Bruce Sanders

Franklin Watts
London • Sydney

Paperback edition published in 2006.

© Aladdin Books Ltd 2003

Designed and produced by
Aladdin Books Ltd
2/3 Fitzroy Mews
London W1T 6DF

First published in Great Britain
in 2003 by
Franklin Watts
338 Euston Road
London NW1 3BH

Franklin Watts Australia
Hachette Children's Books
Level 17/207 Kent Street
Sydney NSW 2000

ISBN: 978-0-7496-7005-4

Design: Flick, Book Design and Graphics
Picture research: Brian Hunter Smart

The consultant, Rohini Kochar, is Education
Officer (Race Equality) for Warwickshire
County Council.

The publishers would like to acknowledge
that the photographs reproduced in this
book have been posed by models or have
been obtained from photographic agencies.

A CIP record for this book is
available from the British Library.

Dewey Classification: 305.8

Printed in Malaysia

Contents

"How am I different?"

There is no one exactly like you. You might share the same colour skin, hair or eyes as a member of your family, or even a friend, but you probably think, feel and behave differently in many ways. The differences between people make life interesting and exciting. Most of us enjoy finding out how other people are different.

But some people treat others unfairly or worse because they have a different skin colour, culture or religion. This is called racism. This book explains how and why racism occurs. If you are being treated unfairly or know someone who is, it gives you some ideas on how to deal with racism.

Life is more exciting because we aren't all exactly the same.

"Where does the word 'racism' come from?"

Someone you know may have a different skin colour to you or they may come from a different country. They might speak a different language, or they might celebrate festivals and wear certain clothes that are part of their religion or culture. Any of these things can make them members of an 'ethnic group'.

Jewish boys and men may wear a skullcap as part of their beliefs.

But whatever ethnic group someone comes from, they and everyone else belong to just one race, the human race.

Yet, because the human race is so varied, people in the past thought of us as many different 'races'. They often used this as an excuse to treat others badly, giving us the word 'racism'.

Think about it

We live in a world where communities are often made up of different ethnic groups. Many people also have parents from different ethnic groups. But we should see every person as an individual, not just as part of a group.

"What is racism?"

Racism is any form of action that is intended to hurt, offend or unfairly treat someone because of their ethnic background.

Treating someone unfairly or calling them names because of their skin colour is the most common form of racism.

Racism is when people are treated badly because of their skin colour, culture or religion.

However, racism isn't just about skin colour. Treating someone badly or unfairly because they belong to a different culture, with a different religion or different ways of doing things, is also racist behaviour.

My story

"My family moved to London from Dublin. Some boys at my new school kept making jokes about me being Irish. They made it really hard to join in." Sean

"Why talk about racism?"

Racism is more than just a problem between two or three people. Racism occurs between cultures, religions and ethnic groups all over the world. It creates problems between different groups of people who could live together in peace and learn from each other. It can make families feel unwelcome or even afraid of attack.

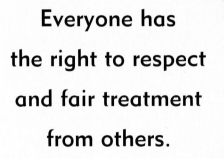

Everyone has the right to respect and fair treatment from others.

Racism can also make it hard for people from some cultures to get jobs, to find a home or to do well in school. There are laws against racism, but it can be hard to prove what has happened.

However it occurs, racism should never be ignored.

Think about it

Many terrible wars have been caused by racism. Today, there is still a great deal of racial conflict around the world. Learning what other people are really like and trying to understand their point of view can help put an end to racism.

"What is prejudice?"

Prejudice is forming an opinion before knowing the facts. Has anyone ever said something like, "You're just like your sister"? Even if you look the same, you both know you're different. When people are racist, they often make up their minds about people based on how they look, rather than getting to know them as individuals.

No one can tell what someone is like just from their culture, skin colour or religion.

If people say things like, "He is Asian, so he must be good at science", it shows they have not bothered to get to know the person they are talking about. They have a point of view based on a fixed idea, or 'stereotype', of Asian people.

Think about it

Stereotypes are ways of thinking about an entire group of people. But it is wrong to think that every member of a group is the same. We are all unique and have different strengths and weaknesses.

"Where do racist ideas come from?"

No one is born racist. They usually get their ideas from other people. Many racist ideas are very old. Hundreds of years ago, people from Europe took control of lands in Asia, America, Africa and Australia. They treated the people already living there very badly and made up stories about them to justify their behaviour.

The stories were passed on, and people believed they were true. This is how stereotypes develop. People believe and repeat racist ideas without finding out whether or not they are true.

My Story

"My uncle loved telling rude jokes about people from other cultures. It made me upset because he was talking about some of my friends. In the end, I told him how I felt. I think he was embarrassed because he's stopped telling the jokes."

Amy

People are not born racist. They learn racist ideas and stereotypes from other people.

"Why are people racist?"

Some people are afraid of things that are new to them. When they don't know about a culture or religion, they may believe bad things they have heard about it.

They may think that their culture or religion is best and that anything different is bad. This may make them treat people from other ethnic backgrounds unfairly.

This Muslim girl is proud of her culture. But some people are afraid of her religion, Islam, because they do not understand it.

People who are racist often refuse to find out for themselves what other cultures are like.

If someone you know is being racist, let them know you do not agree with them. They may stop to think about what they are doing or saying.

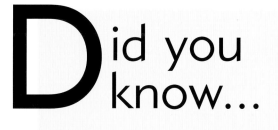

Did you know...

People also use racism to blame others for their own problems or failures. When they see someone from another culture who is successful, like this businessman, they may attack his culture to make themselves feel better.

"How are people racist?"

Racism is a form of bullying, and there are many different ways in which people can be racist.

It is racist to call a person a rude name just because they come from a different culture or country, or because they have a different skin colour.

Being ignored or left out can be just as hurtful as being called names.

Racism can also be ignoring someone or leaving him or her out of a game because of their culture or colour.

To make themselves feel important, some people try to make others feel as if they don't belong.

People can also be racist by making fun of how other people talk or dress. They may say they are just teasing, but it isn't teasing if it upsets or offends the other person.

My story

"When I got into the football team this girl said I only got in because I was black. She was just jealous because she didn't get picked herself, but it really upset me. I want to be in the team because I'm good at football, not because of my skin colour."
Angela

"What about gangs?"

It can be exciting to be in a gang. But racism and bullying often take place when people get into groups. Some groups pick on people from other cultures to make themselves feel better or stronger. People often go along with others in the gang because they are worried they might be picked on themselves.

Fighting back can make things worse, especially if a gang is picking on you.

It can be hard to disagree with everyone else in the gang. But if you are not happy with what they are saying or doing, then you should think about how you can leave it.

If the gang is making life miserable for others, you should also think about letting an adult know what is going on.

Did you know...

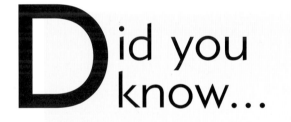

It isn't easy to deal with racist gangs. It is often best to walk away from a situation. But make sure you tell a grown-up what is going on.

Even if you have friends with you, don't fight back if you can help it. You could make things worse, or get blamed for starting the trouble. When people form rival gangs, it often leads to violence.

"How does racism make people feel?"

When someone says or does something racist, it can make the person they are picking on feel angry, sad or lonely.

They may be scared to leave their home or they may skip school to avoid being bullied. They may also find it hard to sleep or may have nightmares.

No one deserves to be bullied because of their skin colour, religion or culture.

If someone is picking on you, you may feel bad about yourself. Try not to listen to what they are saying. It is they, and not you, who are causing the problem. They don't understand what they are saying because they haven't bothered to find out what you, your culture or your religion are really like.

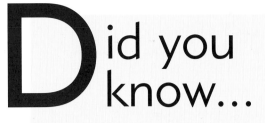

Did you know...

Racist behaviour is a big problem and affects people young and old, at home, at work, at school and in public. It is the cause of many problems in communities and can make people feel afraid, unwelcome or left out.

"How can I deal with racism?"

Being called racist names may make you feel very angry. But if you fight back, it may make things worse. There are other ways to deal with racism:

① You can still stand up for yourself. Tell the bully to leave you alone, then walk away.

② Tell an adult what is going on. We all need help at times.

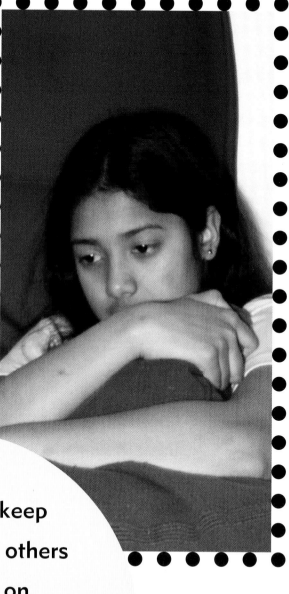

It may help to keep a diary, to show others what is going on.

③ Keep safe and stay close to your friends. Bullies tend to pick on people who are on their own.

④ Never blame yourself. Racism is always wrong.

⑤ Let all your friends know what is happening. When people get together it is easier to find a way of solving the problem.

My story

"This gang at school used to call me racist names and left rude notes on my desk. My friend said she got notes from them, too. At first, we were afraid to tell an adult. But the notes just got worse and worse. So, we showed the notes to our teacher to make it clear what was going on. The gang soon stopped picking on us."
Suhail

"How can I help a friend?"

If you have a friend who is being treated unfairly, the most important thing you can do is speak up for them. If you say nothing, it will look as if you agree with the racists. Your friend may feel that no one is taking their problem seriously. You can help by listening to them talk about what is happening and how they feel.

Racism is a big problem and affects many people. It is not easy to stop racism on your own. Think who might be a good person to tell what is going on.

Talk about it

Your friend may be afraid of talking to anyone else. Encourage them to tell an adult and be willing to back them up. If you don't want to get involved, then let someone else know what is happening.

It's hard to make a stand against racists. You may be scared that they will pick on you instead. But if no one says anything, the bullying could go on for a long time.

Let friends know you are there for them and are willing to help.

"How can we beat racism together?"

School should be a safe place for everyone. You can work together with your friends, teachers and parents to keep it that way. There are laws against racism, and schools have a duty to help. If there are racist bullies or gangs at your school, tell a teacher what is going on, even if it is happening outside school.

Talk to a teacher you trust. Most will listen and will want to help.

Teachers may not realise what is going on when they are not around. Let them know, and tell your parents and friends, so they can support you, too.

Once everyone knows, they should do their best to stop it. Most people find racism and bullying totally unacceptable

My story

"In our school we work together to beat racism. We learn from each other about different cultures and ways of doing things. Last week my friend May showed everyone how to use chopsticks. I wasn't very good, but it was fun!"
Dina

"What can I do?"

• If people are being racist to you, judge when to stand up for yourself, when to leave quickly and when to get help.

• If you have ever said or done anything racist, think about why you did it, and about how hurtful it can be to others.

• We are all part of one race, the human race. Racism only divides us and causes hatred and violence. It is caused by fear, when people do not understand other cultures. Be open to other people, and enjoy finding out about other ways of living.

Life is more fun when we enjoy our differences.

Books on Racism

If you would like to read more on racism, try:

Roll of Thunder, Hear My Cry by Mildred D. Taylor (Addison Wesley)

The Cay by Theodore Taylor (Longman)

Just the Facts: Racism by Adrian Cooper et al (Heineman Library)

Persecution & Prejudice by Bernard J. Dady (Hodder & Stroughton)

Contact information

If you would like to talk to someone who doesn't know you, these organisations can help:

Childline
Tel: 0800 1111
A 24-hour free helpline for children.

Commission for Racial Equality
201-211 Borough High Street,
London, SE1 1GZ
Tel: 020 7939 0000
Email: info@cre.gov
Promotes equality and confronts discrimination.

Minority Rights Group
379 Brixton Road, London, SW9 7DE
Tel: 020 7978 9498
Email: minority.rights@mrgmail.org
Works to secure the rights of minority groups.

On the Web

These websites are also helpful:

www.britkid.org.uk

www.cre.gov.uk

www.minorityrights.org

www.childline.org.uk

www.sikhkids.com

www.bullying.org

www.racismnoway.com.au

www.kidshelp.com.au

The Monitoring
Group,
Emergency Helpline
Tel: 0800 374 618
Support and assistance for victims of racial harrassment.

Kids Helpline, Australia
Tel: 1800 55 1800
A 24-hour free helpline for children.

Racism No Way! Australia
PO Box 590, Darlinghurst, NSW 2010
Email: webkeeper@racismnoway.com.au
Recognition and address of racism in the learning environment.

You can find out more about ways to stop racism in books and on the internet.

Index

Photocredits

Abbreviations: l-left, r-right, b-bottom, t-top, c-centre, m-middle, ba-background
Front cover, 3tr, 26 — Image 100. 1, 6, 7, 16, 22, 23, 25, 28, 30 — Corbis. 2, 3mr, 3br, 4b, 12, 14, 15, 18, 19, 27, 29 — Brand X Pictures. 5b — Digital Stock. 8, 20, 21, 24 — PBD. 9 — Marie-Helene Bradley. 10 — Digital Vision. 11 — Corel. 17 — Flat Earth. 13 — Johnson Space Centre/NASA.